C000132675

From:

WWJD?

What Would Jesus Do?

Written and compiled by
Angela Batchelor

INSPIRE

No challenge; no change
A. B.

Inspire Books is an imprint of Peter Pauper Press, Inc.
Spire is a registered trademark of Peter Pauper Press, Inc.

Designed by Karine Syvertsen

Visit us at www.peterpauper.com

WWJD?

What Would Jesus Do?

CONTENTS

Introduction 5

Recognize Who's
in Charge 8

Choose the Best Way . . . 22

See Others Through
God's Eyes 41

Do Unto Others—
As Jesus Would Do . . . 62

INTRODUCTION

In 1896 a young minister disguised himself as a homeless person and tramped the streets of Topeka, Kansas, asking for help. But no one seemed to care. So the young minister wrote a short novel that challenged his congregation to look at every decision they made through Jesus' eyes. Charles Sheldon's book *In His Steps* summoned his congregants to ask themselves

"What would Jesus do?" when faced with a moment of decision that could influence society.

Those four words still challenge us to see others through God's eyes and do unto others as Jesus would do. When confronted with road rage, work stress, or harsh words—What would Jesus do? When you find spare time, see someone in trouble, or receive an unexpected gift—What would Jesus do? Four words can guide your thoughts and actions. Four words can change your life. Four words: *What would Jesus do*?

To follow in Jesus' footsteps—walk, talk, live, and love like Him—we need to Recognize Who's in Charge, Choose the Best Way, See Others Through God's Eyes, and Do Unto Others—As Jesus Would Do.

—A. B.

RECOGNIZE WHO'S IN CHARGE

If we remember God is the all-powerful creator, who knows and controls all things—nature, humanity—we can harness the power of God within us when we face different situations.

I can do everything through him who gives me strength.

PHILIPPIANS 4:13, NIV

In Jesus our weakness is made perfect.

Peter was a fisherman, who had never found coins in the mouth of a fish. Great faith required him to go and catch one fish to find the exact amount for the tax! He acted on his faith and God provided. When we are in need, God makes provisions out of the blue.

But we don't want to offend these people. So go to the lake and drop in a line; pull up the first fish you hook, and in its mouth you will find a coin worth enough for my temple tax and yours; take it and pay them our taxes.

MATTHEW 17:27, TEV

The Worry Wart

All day Olivia obsessed about her family, finances, and life. Sometimes she lay awake at night thinking about all the things that could go wrong or harm her family. She was concerned about having enough food for the week, having a spotless home, and saving money to send the children to college.

Jesus says we are not to be

anxious about necessities, but find courage to abandon our lives to God's care. Don't worry about today or what you will eat or wear: God will provide. He has provided in the past and He will provide again.

And why worry about clothes? Look how the wild flowers grow; they do not work or make clothes for themselves. . . . It is God who clothes the wild grass— grass that is here today, gone tomorrow, burned up in the oven. Won't he be all the more sure to clothe you? How little faith you have!

Matthew 6:28, 30 TEV

14

In a time of crisis, when the situation seems bleak and daunting with no possible way out, remembering God's past work in our lives is a good way to stay focused and forge ahead.

We humans want to do things our way. We have too much stubbornness, too much independence, and too much self-reliance, causing us to forget God is our shepherd. The Bible calls us sheep: sheep need supervision. They won't drink from running water and get dehydrated walking by a stream; they need someone to lead them to a pool. We aren't always conscious of our shepherd's aid and direction either. Yet He leads, not drives, us where He needs us to be.

I am the good shepherd.
The good shepherd gives
His life for the sheep.

JOHN 10:11, NKJV

Part of our capacity to endure stressful events is to know we are being strengthened and prepared by our failures. As Corrie ten Boom notes about her memories of life in a Nazi concentration camp: "Every experience God gives us, every person He puts in our lives, is the perfect preparation for the future that only He can see."

Belief and trust in God
can move mountains.
Don't be discouraged
by circumstances.

He replied, "Because you have so little faith. I tell you the truth, if you have faith as small as a mustard seed, you can say to this mountain, 'Move from here to there' and it will move. Nothing will be impossible for you."

MATTHEW 17:20, NIV

There is nothing
that wastes the body
like worry, and one
who has any faith in
God should be ashamed
to worry about
anything whatsoever.

Mahatma Gandhi

CHOOSE THE
BEST WAY

Jesus did not choose between good and bad; he chose between better and best. He resisted temptation, put away His pride and focused on His purpose.

It is better to take refuge in the LORD than to trust in man.

PSALM 118: 8, NIV

We cannot find our mission until we understand ourselves. Even Jesus had to go out into the wilderness to clarify who He was and to concentrate on His gifts. Afterwards, He was able to tell himself and others, with great confidence, self-knowledge, and self-esteem, who He was. He said, "I am the Light. I am the Way. I am the Vine. I am the Good Shepherd. I am the Gate."

When we live life centered around what others like, feel, and say, we lose touch with our identity. I am an eternal being, created by God. I am an individual with purpose. It's not what I get from life, but who I am, that makes the difference.

NEVA COYLE

Look at what I am here to do. Then choose the best. Apply this strategy for jobs, career, relationships, and ministry.

When Jesus visited His
friends Mary and Martha
in Bethany both sisters served
Him. Mary decided to sit at
His feet and listen to His word.
Martha busied herself with
household chores and food
preparation. Annoyed, Martha
asked Jesus if Mary should
not help as well. Jesus replied,
"But one thing is needed, and
Mary has chosen that good

part, which will not be taken away from her."(Luke 10:42, NKJV)

Remember that insults, slights, harsh words say more about the other person than about you, so choose the best response.

*Father, forgive them,
for they do not know
what they are doing.*

LUKE 23:34, NIV

*A fool's wrath is presently
known: but a prudent
man covereth shame.*

PROVERBS 12:16 KJV

Be morally courageous. Act with integrity. Give to God what is right, good, compassionate. Don't steal or cheat. Depend on inner heart health to help you do, think, and believe. Truly, that's more important than what you say.

What we truly are will dictate our choices, no matter how we try to camouflage or hide it, and no amount of moral effort will make us choose rightly if our hearts aren't right. Sooner or later the pressures and pace of our lives will expose what we really are.

GLORIA GAITHER

Wield your power wisely. Let love be your aim. Otherwise you'll be like Pilate and yield your ethics to peer pressure.

Love is patient and kind.
Love is not jealous or boast-
ful or proud or rude. Love
does not demand its own
way. Love is not irritable,
and it keeps no record of
when it has been wronged.

1 Corinthians 13:4-5, NLT

Let love be your aim and make the good better, the ordinary extraordinary. Jesus made water into wine, hugged children, healed the sick, and washed the feet of his disciples.

As chefs plate beautiful food, so we can serve macaroni and cheese on china.

We're good at giving, but to choose the best, sometimes we have to receive. We need to work on embracing the gift of God's love and affirmation, whether it comes as a hug, a gift, a compliment, or allowing someone else to help us. Sheep were never meant to carry burdens like donkeys or horses. And the Bible calls us sheep.

Come unto me, all ye that labour and are heavy laden, and I will give you rest.

MATTHEW 11:28 KJV

We may also need to seek out a simpler lifestyle: the Bible says Jesus had no place to lay his head. We may be called to "live more simply so that others can simply live."

If anyone has material possessions and sees his brother in need but has no pity on him, how can the love of God be in him?
Dear children, let us not love with words or tongue but with actions and in truth.

1 John 3:17-18, NIV

Consider: Would Jesus wear a Rolex, drive a fancy car? Would He give up some of His affluence to feed the poor? Gear down from the fast track to find time to help others?

Why spend money on what is not bread, and your labor on what does not satisfy? Listen, listen to me, and eat what is good, and your soul will delight in the richest of fare.

ISAIAH 55:2, NIV

God holds the future
in His hands
With grace sufficient
day by day,
Through good or ill
He gently leads,
If we but let Him
have His way.

ROHRS

SEE OTHERS THROUGH GOD'S EYES

God sees us as a uniquely beautiful people that He cares for "as the apple of His eye." When we learn the art of seeing with the same generosity, mercy and love as God does we develop a new perspective—on ourselves, other people, and the whole universe.

Do not grow accustomed to homelessness and hardship. Do not just look out for number one, but learn to look for those who are lost. Jesus tells the story of the lost coin, lost sheep, and lost son. His love was so great that He searched for each one and rejoiced when they were found.

You have not taken
care of the weak. You have
not tended the sick or bound
up the broken bones. You
have not gone looking
for those who have wandered
away and are lost. Instead,
you have ruled them with
force and cruelty.

EZEKIEL 34:4, NLT

We have lost values in our churches, culture, community, country, families, and religion.

**From what we get,
we can make a living;
what we give,
however, makes a life.**

ARTHUR ASHE

Racism shuts out more than just others—it shuts out God, too. Remember that each person is sacramental, a holy creation, God's child.

So God created people
in his own image;
God patterned them
after himself;
male and female he
created them.

GENESIS 1:27 NLT

Artists see from a different perspective. We need God's perspective to see into human hearts.

We need to find and see the true worth of each individual self—not judge on race, creed, status. When we do, we can help the powerless feel more powerful.

A person is a person
because he recognizes
others as persons.

BISHOP DESMOND TUTU

If you want to lift
yourself up, lift up
someone else.

BOOKER T. WASHINGTON

Peter denied Jesus three times, yet Jesus chose Peter as the foundation for the church; Jesus saw something in Peter that others had missed.

Pay attention to the intent, motives, and progress of an individual. Look for a deeper vision. Small starts can bring great rewards.

Look at the mistakes of others with eyes of compassion, not judgment. Don't contribute further to their downfall. Most people are already their own worst critics. Remember that when we live in glass houses we shouldn't throw stones.

There is power in little things: a whole tree comes from an apple seed.

When an irritating co-worker wreaks havoc on your day, think of him as wood and yourself as God's sandpaper. Sandpaper can be used to smooth out wood. With this in mind, you will respond to your co-worker in a helpful manner.

The LORD does not look at the things man looks at. Man looks at the outward appearance, but the LORD looks at the heart.

1 Samuel 16:7, NIV

Do not judge according to appearance, but judge with righteous judgment.

JOHN 7:24, NKJV

No finger pointing; no blame game. Instead look, love, laugh. Help others see their potential for wisdom, knowledge, confidence, faith. Jesus transformed Paul from skeptic to evangelist, reshaped Mary from prostitute into a model for living.

Rely on God's love and mercy, not judgment, even when it comes to yourself. You will make mistakes, but you don't have to repeat them. Just look at the logs in your own eye before you try to take the speck out of someone else's. Master the art of leading yourself.

*Do not judge, and you
will not be judged;
do not condemn,
and you will not
be condemned.
Forgive, and you
will be forgiven.*

LUKE 6:37, NIV

Jesus knew when to stand tall, when to bend His knee, and when to do both. Look at things the way He does.

He went to Nazareth,
where he had been brought
up, and on the Sabbath day
he went into the synagogue,
as was his custom.
And he stood up to read.

LUKE 4:16, NIV

Take time to pray and read Scripture as He did. Get up early for a quiet time with God.

Very early in the morning, while it was still dark, Jesus got up, left the house and went off to a solitary place, where he prayed.

MARK 1:35, NIV

Do Unto Others—As Jesus Would Do

Be prepared for anything that God sends, without preconceived ideas or agendas. Follow God's instructions.

In the morning,

O LORD, you hear my voice;

in the morning I lay my

requests before you

and wait in expectation.

PSALM 5:3, NIV

In Palestine a wedding feast lasted a week. The bridegroom could have arrived today, tomorrow, or next week. For that reason, the bridesmaids kept the bride company until his arrival, and no one could go out after dark without a lamp.

So Jesus teaches us about preparation using the story about ten bridesmaids being ready before a wedding. Five were wise

and five were foolish. The wise
ones were prepared. They brought
lamps with extra oil. The foolish
ones did not bring extra oil. In
fact, they took a nap. After a long
time, the bridegroom arrived.
The wise ones lit their lamps and
followed him to the wedding
banquet. The foolish ones didn't
have any oil and stumbled along
after them in the dark. But alas,
they didn't arrive until the door

had been shut and they were
unable to participate in the
wedding feast. They were left
out by their own foolishness.

We need to be ever ready to
serve, for Jesus says He will return
like a thief in the night.

Often times our well-laid plans are not God's divine plans. We need to take interruptions, phone calls, and requests to do someone good as God's agenda for our days.

We don't need
to know where we are
going if we let God
do the leading.

Though Jesus was entitled to be treated with respect, He chose to be a servant. Therefore, we should be ready and willing to be used in any way God chooses. You can lead others to God by serving Him.

Who, being in the form of God,
thought it not robbery to be equal
with God: But made himself of
no reputation, and took upon him
the form of a servant, and was
made in the likeness of men: And
being found in fashion as
a man, he humbled himself, and
became obedient unto death, even
the death of the cross.

PHILIPPIANS 2:6-8, KJV

People feel that somebody else "owes" them, that it's their right—but Jesus said "take up your cross" and follow me.

But I tell you not to resist an evil person. But whoever slaps you on your right cheek, turn the other to him also.

MATTHEW 5:39, NKJV

Be about the work of faith. Live as if heaven depended on your service to others. Let your light shine and live what you preach. In other words, "walk the talk."

Remember that grace is a gift with strings attached—heartstrings.

Sometimes, just your presence at a needed time is enough.

Your service should be etched in kindness; kindness is the key to Christ likeness.

Jesus never used threats or intimidation to get things done. He motivated others with mercy and kindness.

Seek first to understand, then to be understood.

STEVEN R. COVEY

A kind man benefits himself, but a cruel man brings himself harm.

PROVERBS 11:17, NIV

We allow too much hatred and unkindness. But those who serve and help solve the problems have little time to criticize or blame others and God.

When you hold onto
the bitterness for years,
it stops you from living
your life fully. As it
turns out, it wears out
your immune system
and hurts your heart.

FRED LUSKIN

Follow the Golden Rule:
treat everyone well—
both the deserving and
the undeserving.

When we follow
Jesus' leadership,
God gets the glory.